COMMUNITY HELPERS

Servers

by Kieran Downs

BLASTOFF! READERS 1

BELLWETHER MEDIA • MINNEAPOLIS, MN

Blastoff! Readers are carefully developed by literacy experts to build reading stamina and move students toward fluency by combining standards-based content with developmentally appropriate text.

Level 1 provides the most support through repetition of high-frequency words, light text, predictable sentence patterns, and strong visual support.

Level 2 offers early readers a bit more challenge through varied sentences, increased text load, and text-supportive special features.

Level 3 advances early-fluent readers toward fluency through increased text load, less reliance on photos, advancing concepts, longer sentences, and more complex special features.

★ **Blastoff! Universe**

Reading Level

Grade K — Blastoff! Beginners

Grades 1–3 — Blastoff! Readers

Grade 4 — Blastoff! Discovery

This edition first published in 2021 by Bellwether Media, Inc.

Library of Congress Cataloging-in-Publication Data

Names: Downs, Kieran, author.
Title: Servers / by Kieran Downs.
Description: Minneapolis : Bellwether Media, 2021. | Series: Blastoff! Readers: Community helpers | Includes bibliographical references and index. | Audience: Ages 5-8 | Audience: Grades K-1 | Summary:"Developed by literacy experts for students in kindergarten through grade three, this book introduces servers to young readers through leveled text and related photos"–Provided by publisher.
Identifiers: LCCN 2019053756 (print) | LCCN 2019053757 (ebook) | ISBN 9781644871966 (library binding) | ISBN 9781681038209 (paperback) | ISBN 9781618919540 (ebook)
Subjects: LCSH: Waiters–Juvenile literature. | Waitresses–Juvenile literature.
Classification: LCC TX925 .D69 2021 (print) | LCC TX925 (ebook) | DDC 642/.6-dc23
LC record available at https://lccn.loc.gov/2019053756
LC ebook record available at https://lccn.loc.gov/2019053757

Editor: Betsy Rathburn   Designer: Laura Sowers

Printed in the United States of America, North Mankato, MN.

Table of Contents

Out to Eat

A family is out to eat.
A server takes
their **order**.

The server writes down
what they want.
She delivers the food
when it is ready!

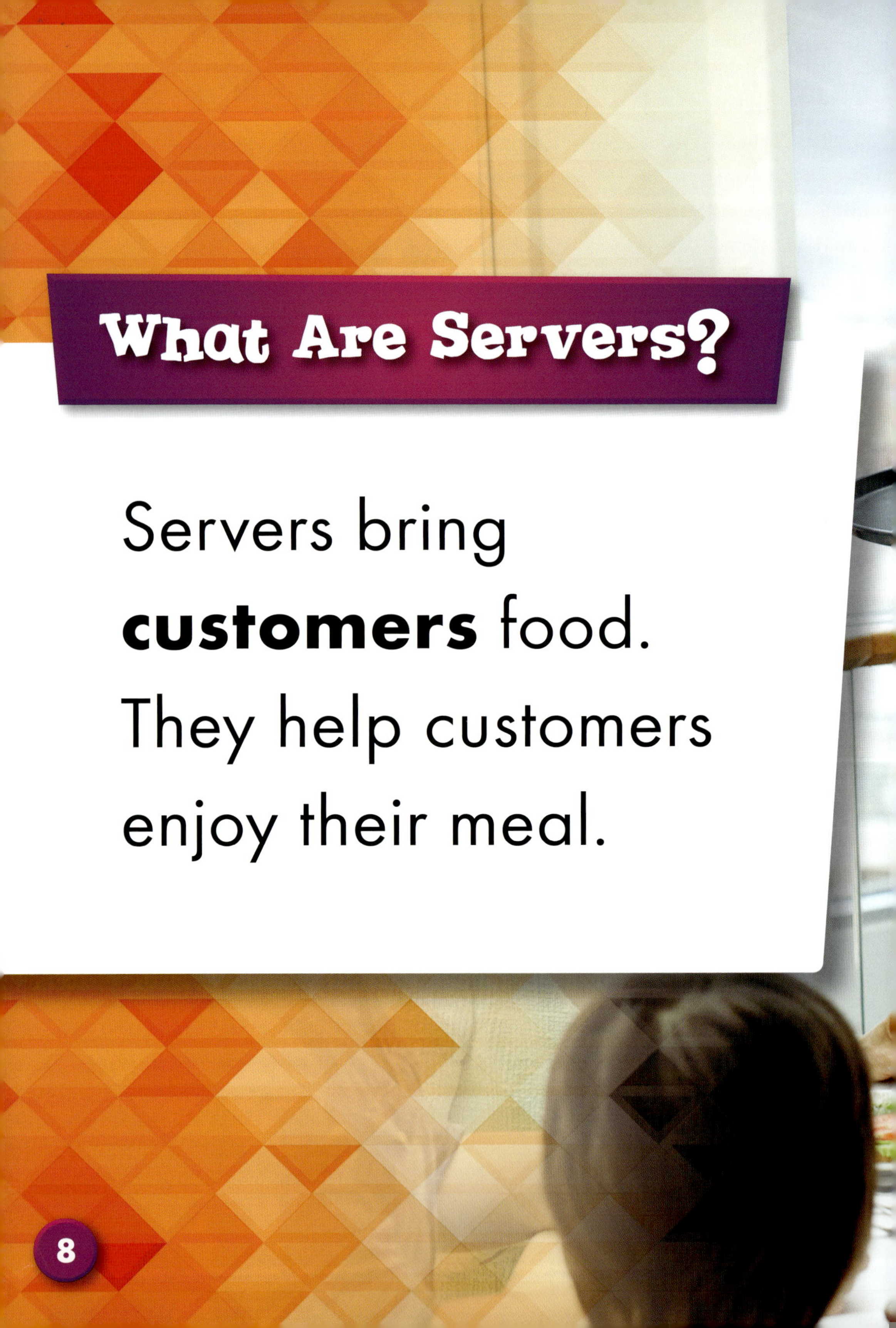

What Are Servers?

Servers bring **customers** food. They help customers enjoy their meal.

customer

Servers work
in **restaurants**.
They mostly work
in the **dining area**.

dining area

What Do Servers Do?

Servers take orders to the kitchen. They also bring customers drinks.

Servers need to know the **menu**. They tell customers about **specials**.

menu

Servers help keep the restaurant clean. They wipe tables and clear dirty dishes.

Server Gear

What Makes a Good Server?

Servers must be good with people. They also need a good memory.

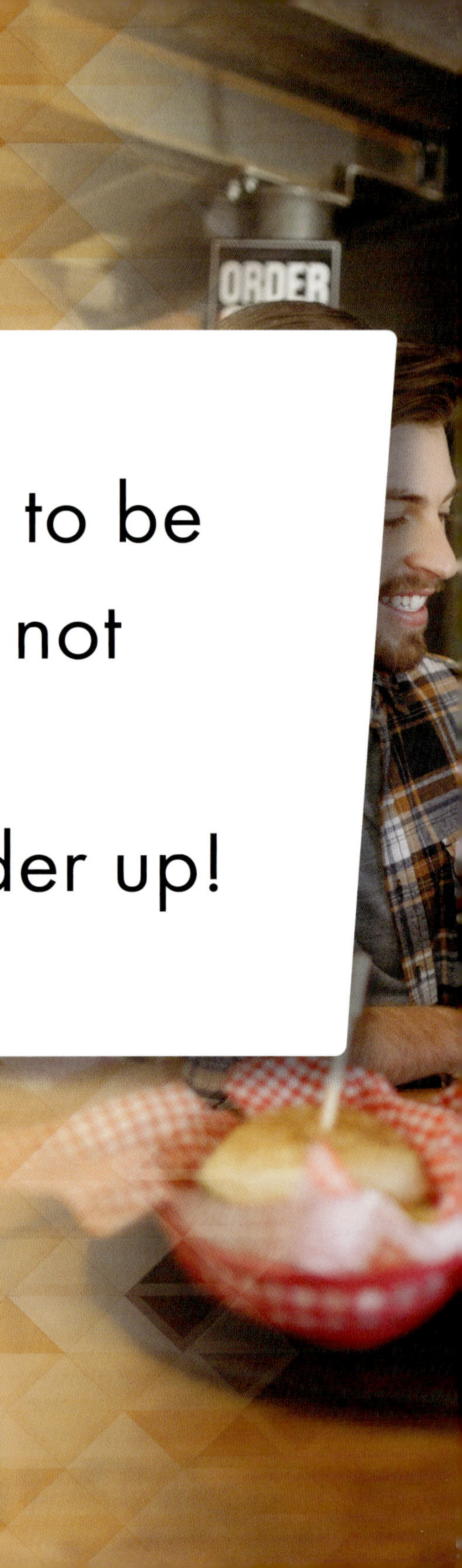

Servers need to be fast. They do not want food to get cold. Order up!

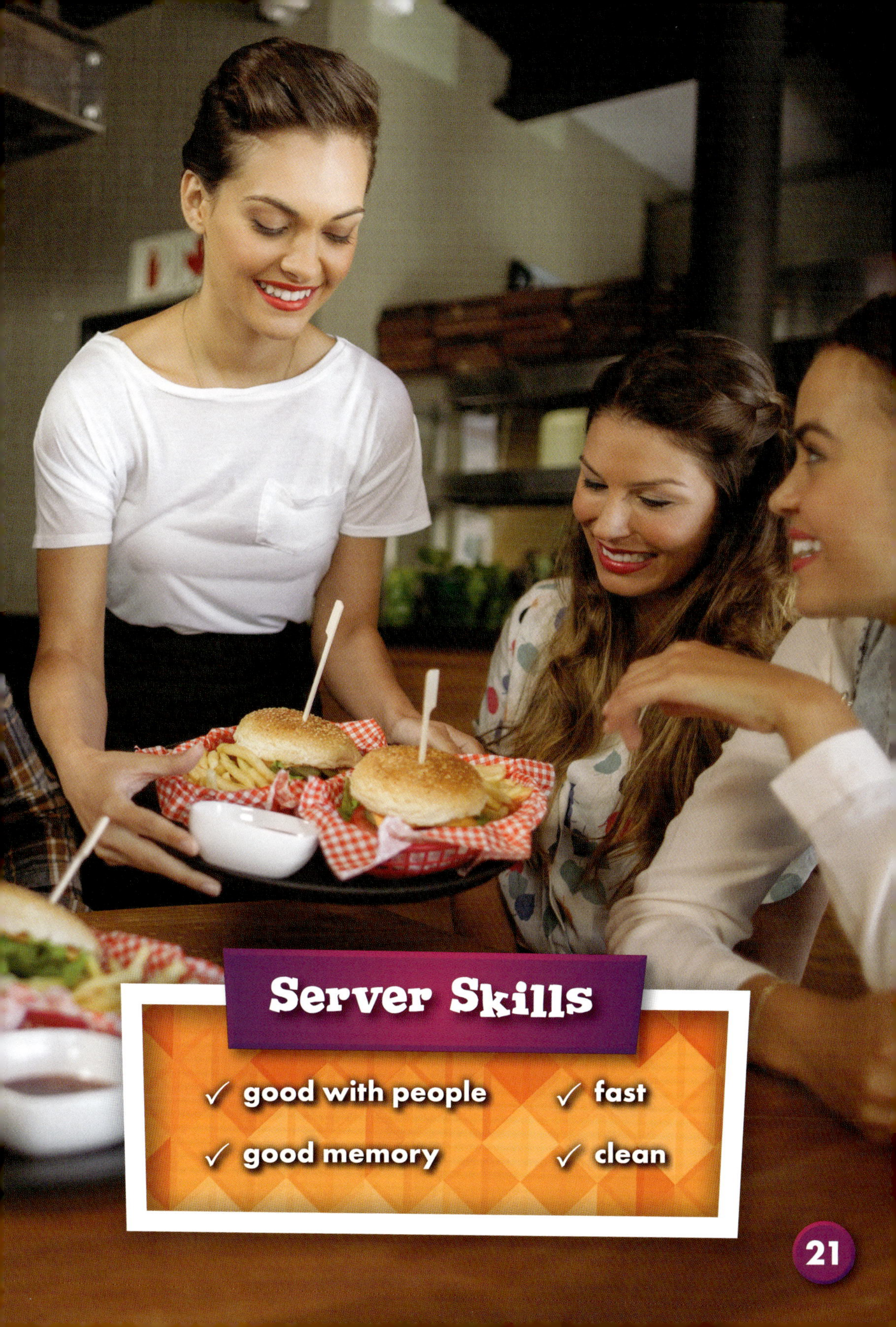

Server Skills

- ✓ good with people
- ✓ fast
- ✓ good memory
- ✓ clean

Glossary

customers

people who pay for goods or services

order

a direction that tells what a person wants

dining area

the place in a restaurant where customers sit

restaurants

places where people can buy meals

menu

a list of food available in a restaurant

specials

items that are not normally on a menu

To Learn More

AT THE LIBRARY

Battista, Brianna. *I Want to Be a Chef.* New York, N.Y.: PowerKids Press, 2018.

Moening, Kate. *Chefs.* Minneapolis, Minn.: Bellwether Media, 2019.

Shores, Erika L. *How Food Gets from Farms to Store Shelves.* North Mankato, Minn.: Capstone Press, 2016.

ON THE WEB

FACTSURFER

Factsurfer.com gives you a safe, fun way to find more information.

1. Go to www.factsurfer.com.
2. Enter "servers" into the search box and click .
3. Select your book cover to see a list of related content.

Index

The images in this book are reproduced through the courtesy of: Pixel-Shot, front cover; Iakov Filimonov, pp. 4-5, 6-7; Pressmaster, pp. 8-9; andresr, pp. 10-11, 18-19; Geber86, pp. 12-13; El Nariz, pp. 14-15; LightField Studios, pp. 16-17; Dmitry Zimin, p. 17 (apron); Dmitrii Kazitsyn, p. 17 (dishrag); Vitaly Zorkin, p. 17 (pencil); eurobanks, p. 17 (paper); Elster, p. 17 (tray); wavebreakmedia, pp. 20-21; Monkey Business Images, p. 22 (top left); Drazen Zigic, p. 22 (top left); Sorbis, p. 22 (middle left); Rawpixel, p. 22 (middle right); BOOCYS, p. 22 (bottom right).